D0525092

THE REVENGE OF THE BABY-SAT

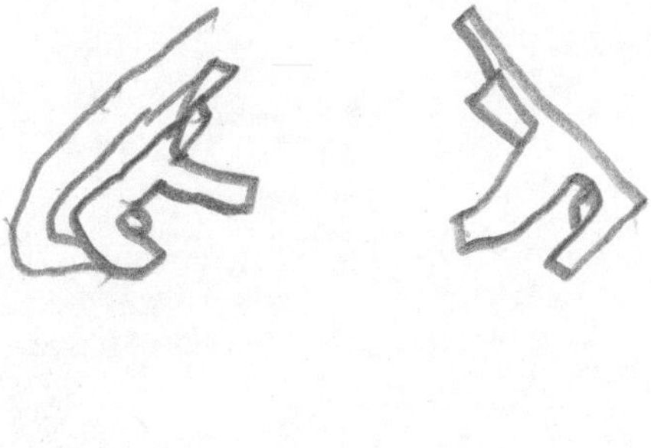

Also by Bill Watterson

Calvin and Hobbes
Something Under the Bed Is Drooling
Yukon Ho!
Weirdos From Another Planet
Lazy Sunday Book
The Authoritative Calvin and Hobbes
Scientific Progress Goes 'Boink'
Attack of the Deranged Mutant Killer Monster Snow Goons

Taken from *Calvin and Hobbes*:

Calvin and Hobbes 1: Thereby Hangs a Tale
Calvin and Hobbes 2: One Day the Wind Will Change
Calvin and Hobbes 3: In the Shadow of the Night

THE REVENGE OF THE BABY-SAT

A Calvin and Hobbes Collection by Bill Watterson

WARNER BOOKS

A *Warner* Book

First published in the US by Andrews and McMeel 1991
First published in Great Britain by Sphere Books Ltd 1991
Reprinted 1991, 1992
This edition published by Warner Books 1992

Printed and bound in Great Britain by
BPCC Hazells Ltd
Member of BPCC Ltd

ISBN 0 7474 0939 0

Warner Books
A Division of
Little, Brown and Company (UK) Limited
165 Great Dover Street
London SE1 4YA

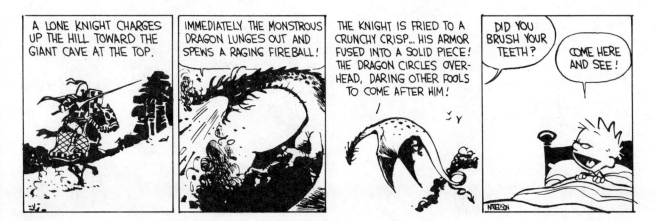

9

11

17

19

21

YES, CAN I HAVE THE TOOL DEPARTMENT, PLEASE? THANK YOU.

HELLO? HOW MUCH ARE YOUR POWER CIRCULAR SAWS? I SEE. AND YOUR ELECTRIC DRILLS? UH-HUH. HOW BIG OF A BIT WILL THAT HOLD? REALLY? GREAT.

SO THE ASSIGNMENT IS PAGES TWO THROUGH FOUR? OK, THANKS SUSIE.

..SORRY ABOUT THAT. DO YOU CARRY ACETYLENE TORCHES? OK, RING IT ALL UP. THIS WILL BE ON MASTERCARD.

LOOK AT ALL THIS HOMEWORK I'M SUPPOSED TO DO!

I DON'T WANT TO DO THIS GARBAGE! I WANT TO GO PLAY OUTSIDE!

CHILDHOOD IS SHORT AND MATURITY IS FOREVER.

PEOPLE ARE ROTTEN.

WHEN I GROW UP, I'M GOING TO LIVE A MILLION MILES AWAY FROM EVERYONE!

HOW WILL YOU SURVIVE? WHAT WILL YOU EAT?

...WELL, MOM COULD COME BY TWICE A DAY TO COOK, I SUPPOSE.

THAT WOULD BE QUITE A COMMUTE.

30

31

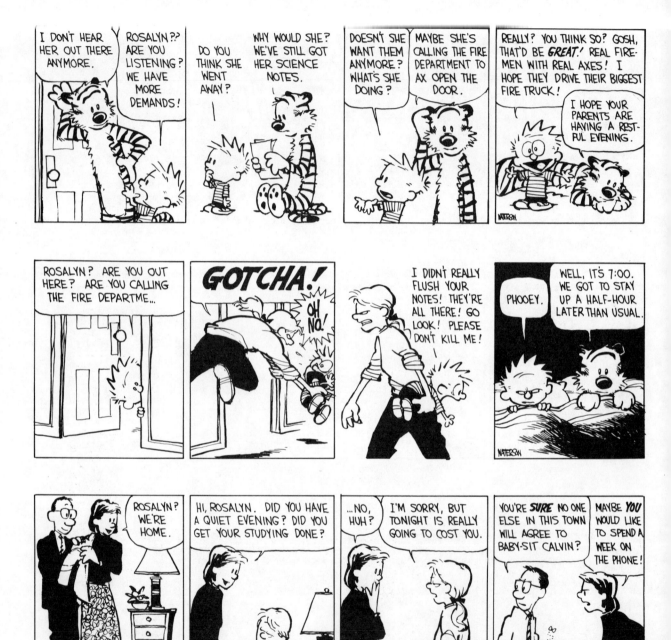

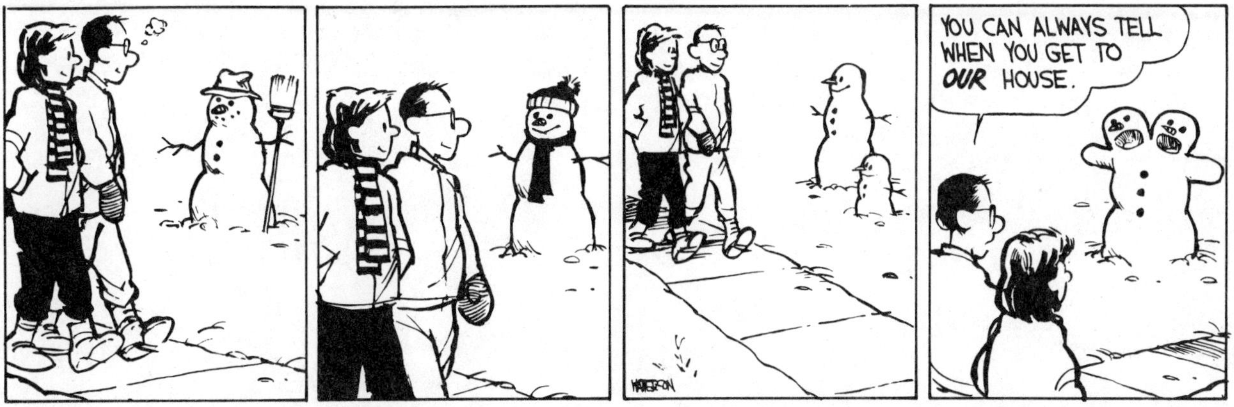
YOU CAN ALWAYS TELL WHEN YOU GET TO OUR HOUSE.

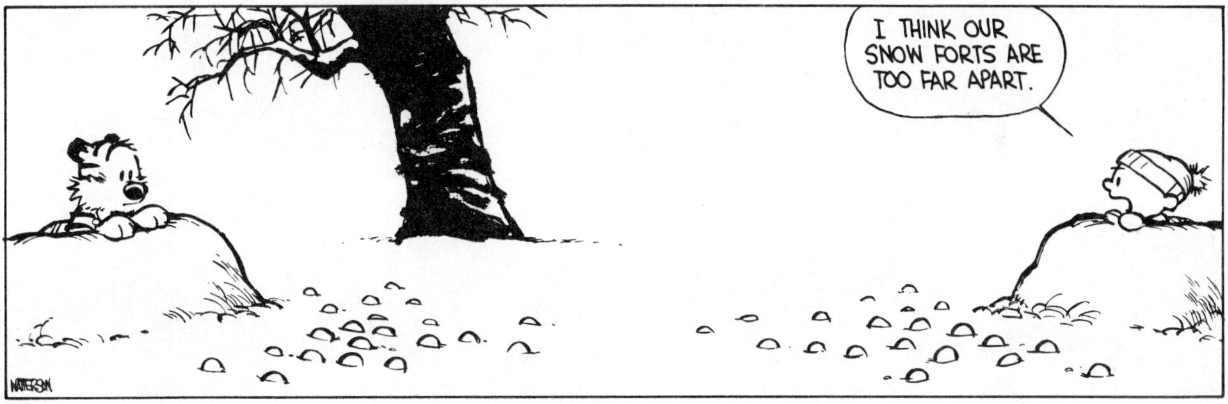
I THINK OUR SNOW FORTS ARE TOO FAR APART.

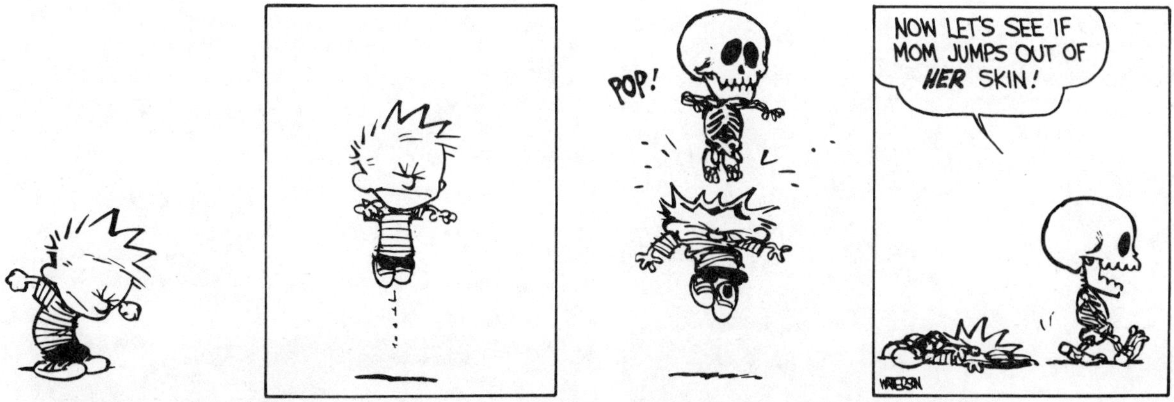
POP!
NOW LET'S SEE IF MOM JUMPS OUT OF HER SKIN!

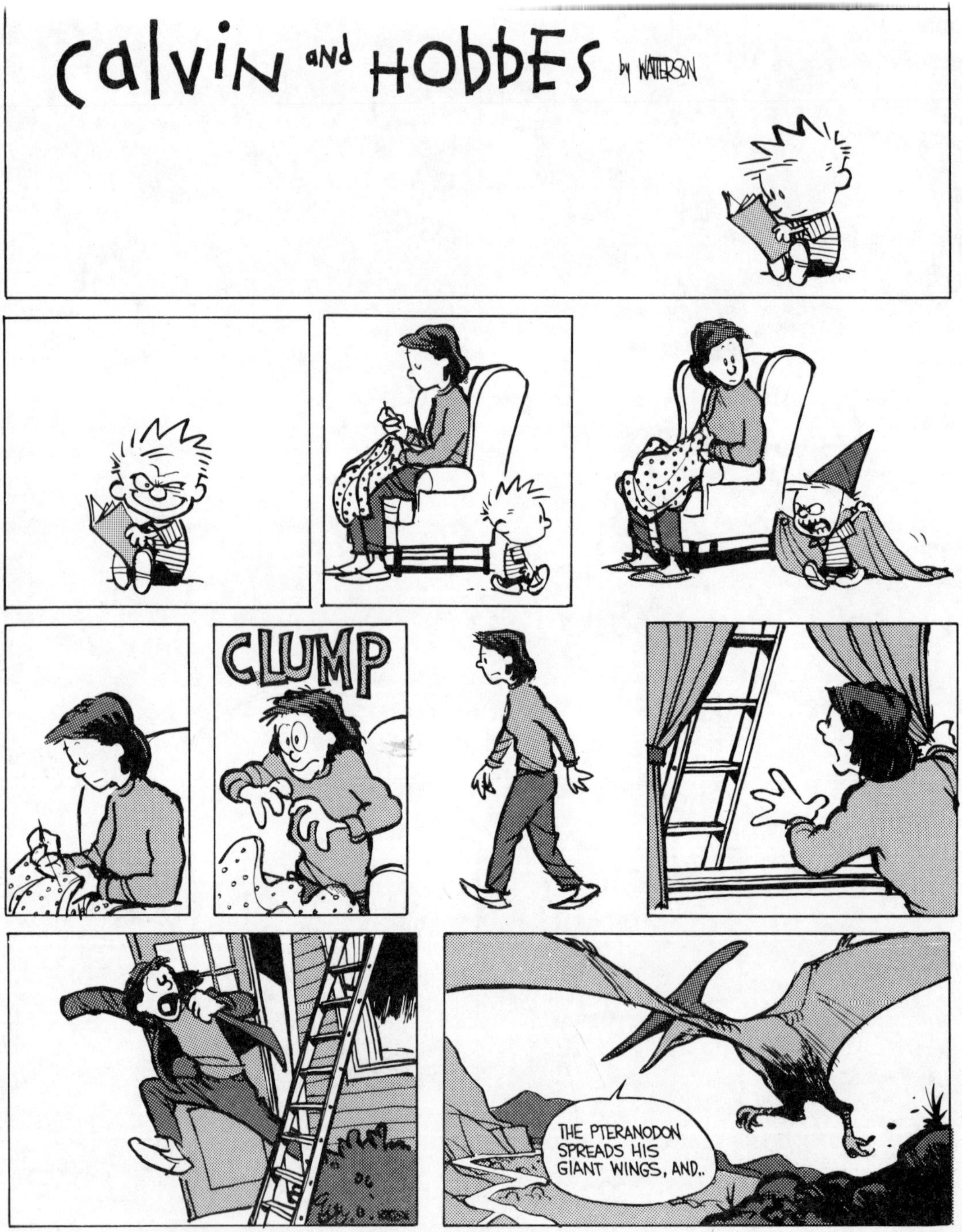
Calvin and HOBBES
by WATTERSON
CLUMP
THE PTERANODON SPREADS HIS GIANT WINGS, AND..

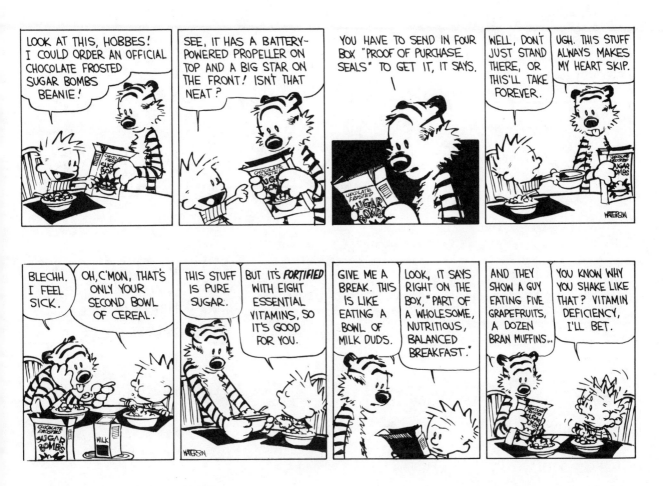

44

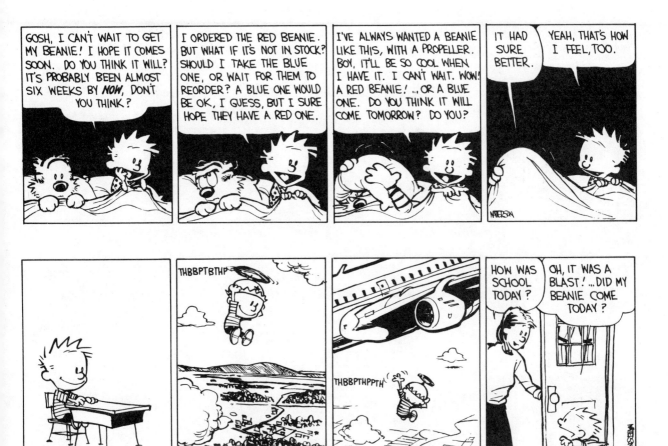

45

46

48

54

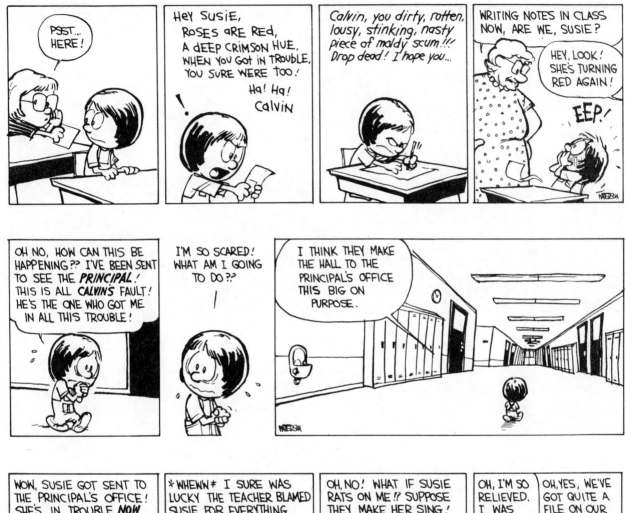

Panel 1: HERE COMES SUSIE, BACK FROM THE PRINCIPAL'S OFFICE. BOY, DOES SHE LOOK PALE. I WONDER WHAT HAPPENED. SHE'S TALKING TO THE TEACHER NOW.

Panel 2: PSST! SUSIE, WHAT DID THEY DO TO YOU? DID YOU GET EXPELLED? YOU DIDN'T SNITCH ON *ME*, DID YOU?

Panel 4: YOU *DID* SNITCH! YOU'RE A *STOOLIE!* A CANARY!

YOU'RE GOING UP THE RIVER, CALVIN.

CALVIN, WILL YOU COME HERE, PLEASE?

Panel 5: SO *FIRST* I GOT IN TROUBLE FOR NOT PAYING ATTENTION IN CLASS AND FOR TURNING IN A LAST-MINUTE INSECT COLLECTION, WHICH I GOT A "D-MINUS-MINUS" ON.

Panel 6: *THEN* I GOT IN TROUBLE FOR GETTING *SUSIE* IN TROUBLE WHEN I WANTED HER TO HELP ME FUDGE THE PROJECT.

Panel 7: *THEN* I GOT IN TROUBLE WHEN I TOLD MOM, AND *THEN* I GOT IN TROUBLE *AGAIN* WHEN *SHE* TOLD *DAD!* I'VE BEEN IN HOT WATER EVER SINCE I GOT UP!

Panel 8: WOW. I'LL BET ALL THIS MAKES YOU GET YOUR BOOK REPORT FINISHED RIGHT ON TIME.

MY WHAT?

Panel 9: ONE OF NATURE'S MOST PECULIAR-LOOKING CREATURES, THE GIRAFFE IS UNIQUELY SUITED TO ITS ENVIRONMENT.

Panel 10: HIS TREMENDOUS HEIGHT ENABLES HIM TO MUNCH ON THE SUCCULENT MORSELS MOST DIFFICULT TO REACH.

Panel 11: COOKIE

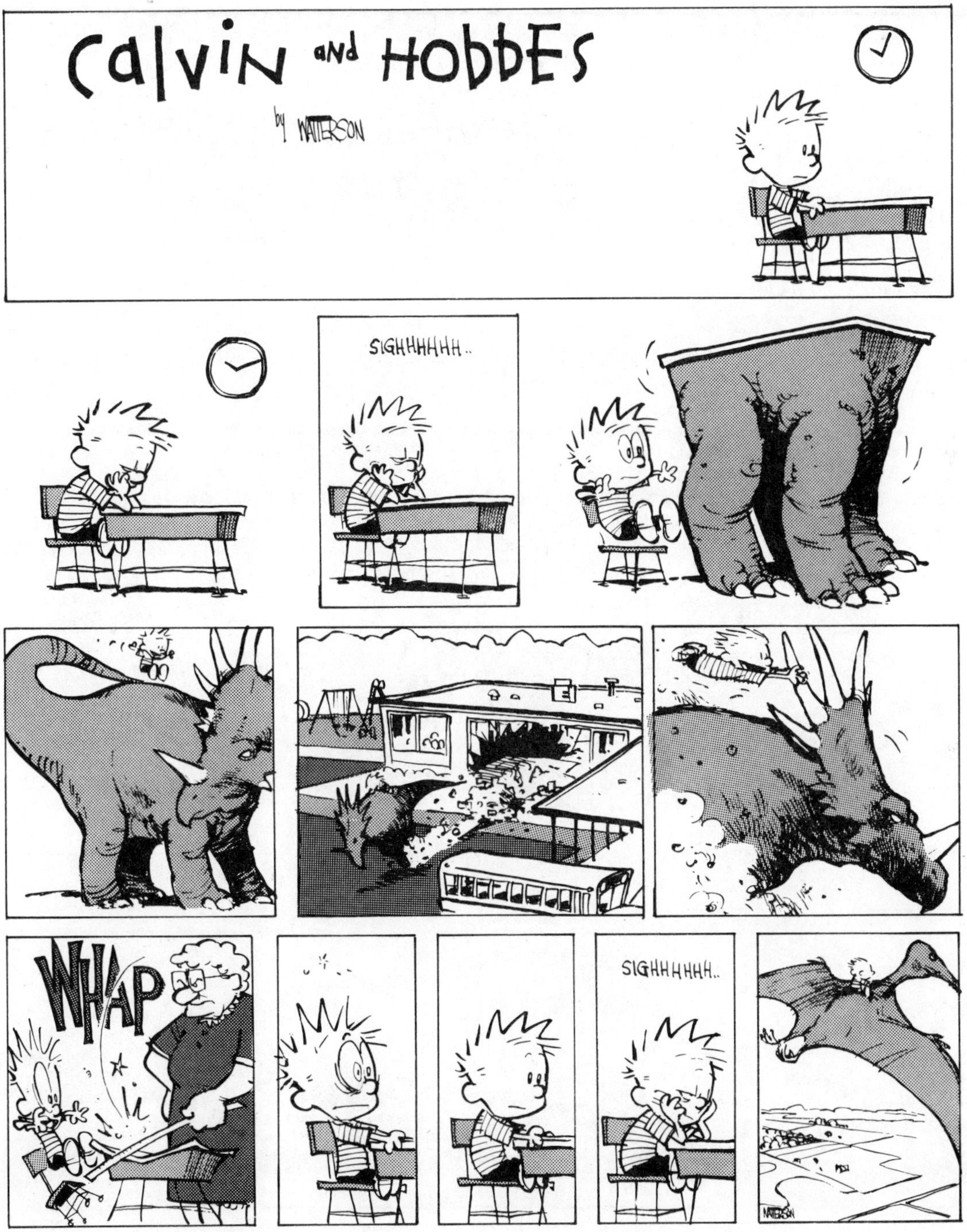
Calvin and HOBBES
by WATTERSON
SIGHHHHHH..
WHAP
SIGHHHHHH..
WATTERSON

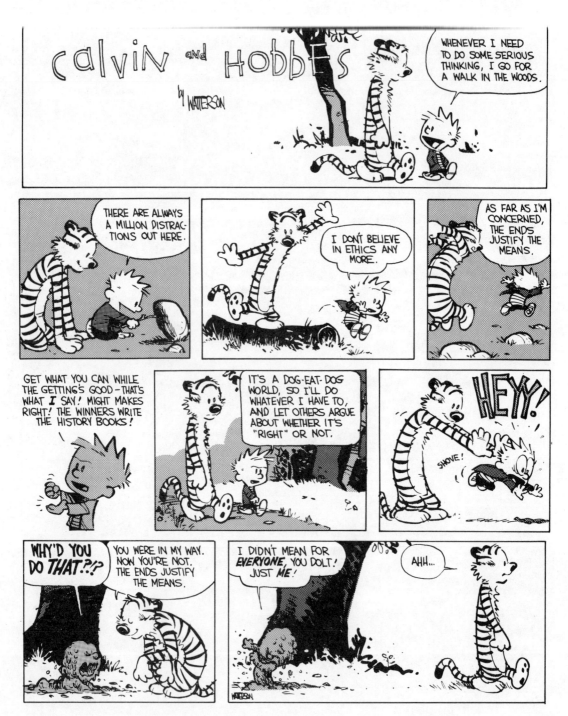

62

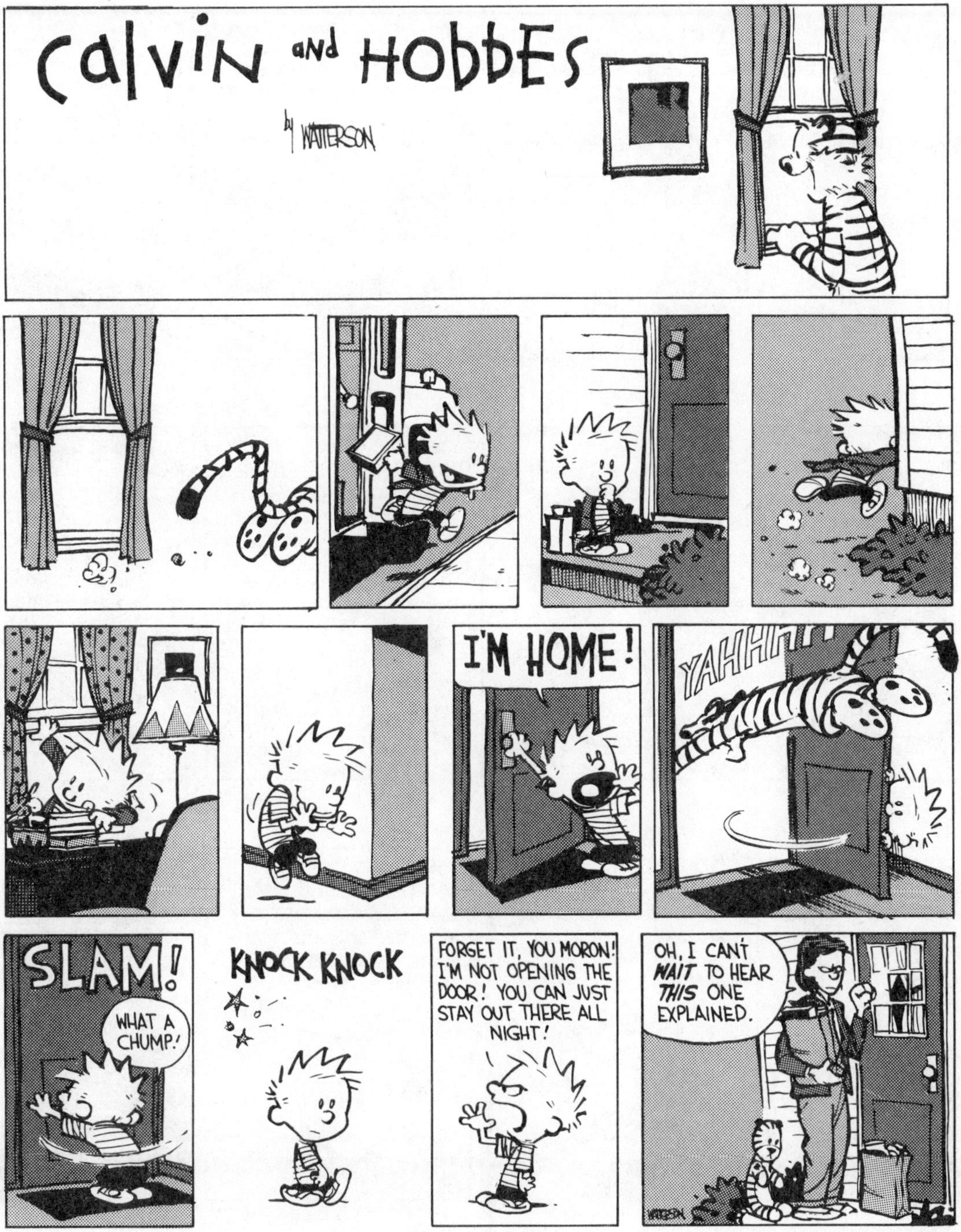
Calvin and HOBBES
by WATTERSON
I'M HOME!
YAHHHH
SLAM!
WHAT A CHUMP!
KNOCK KNOCK
FORGET IT, YOU MORON! I'M NOT OPENING THE DOOR! YOU CAN JUST STAY OUT THERE ALL NIGHT!
OH, I CAN'T WAIT TO HEAR THIS ONE EXPLAINED.
WATTERSON

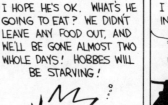

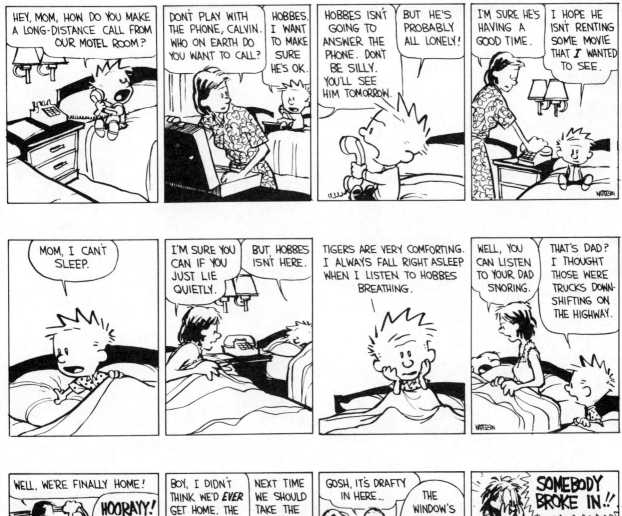

74

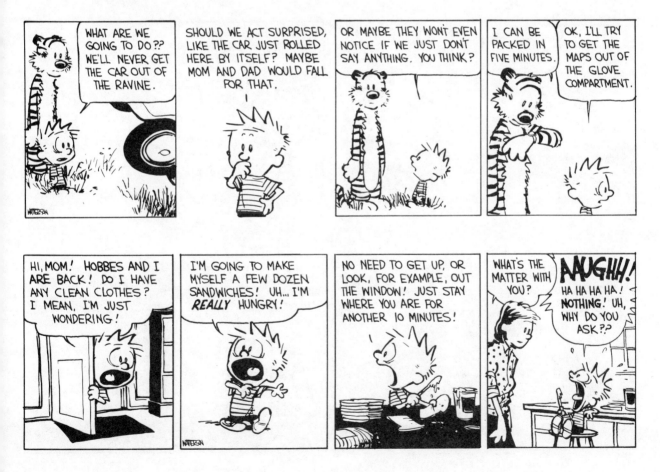

HERE'S THE LATEST POLL OF HOUSEHOLD 6-YEAR-OLDS, DAD.

AN OVERWHELMING MAJORITY EXPRESS AMAZEMENT AT HOW LITTLE YOU'VE ACCOMPLISHED AS DAD SO FAR. THE IMPRESSION IS THAT YOU'RE AVOIDING ALL THE HARD DECISIONS THAT NEED TO BE MADE.

IN FACT, NONE OF THOSE POLLED COULD NAME A SINGLE INSTANCE OF TRUE PATERNAL LEADERSHIP.

HOW ABOUT IF I LEAD YOU UPSTAIRS TO YOUR BED?

HA HA. IF WE CAN BE SERIOUS FOR A MOMENT, I HAVE SOME INNOVATIVE IDEAS ABOUT MY ALLOWANCE.

LOOK AT ALL THESE ANTS.

THEY'RE ALL RUNNING LIKE MAD, WORKING TIRELESSLY ALL DAY, NEVER STOPPING, NEVER RESTING.

AND FOR WHAT? TO BUILD A TINY LITTLE HILL OF SAND THAT COULD BE WIPED OUT AT ANY MOMENT! ALL THEIR WORK COULD BE FOR NOTHING, AND YET THEY KEEP ON BUILDING. THEY NEVER GIVE UP!

I SUPPOSE THERE'S A LESSON IN THAT.

YEAH ... ANTS ARE MORONS. LET'S SEE WHAT'S ON TV.

BOY, WHAT A GROUCH.

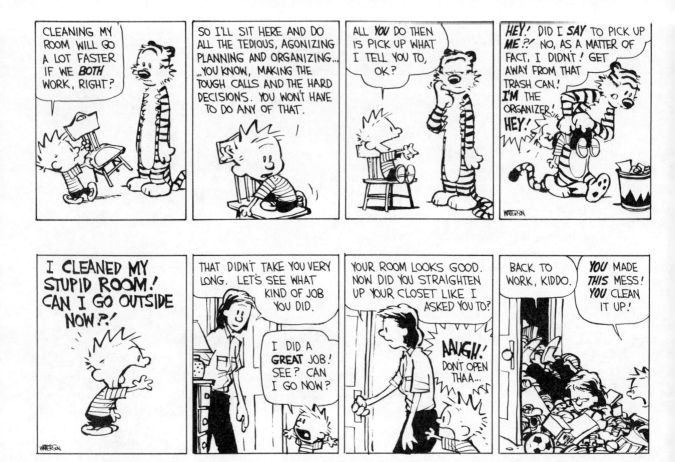

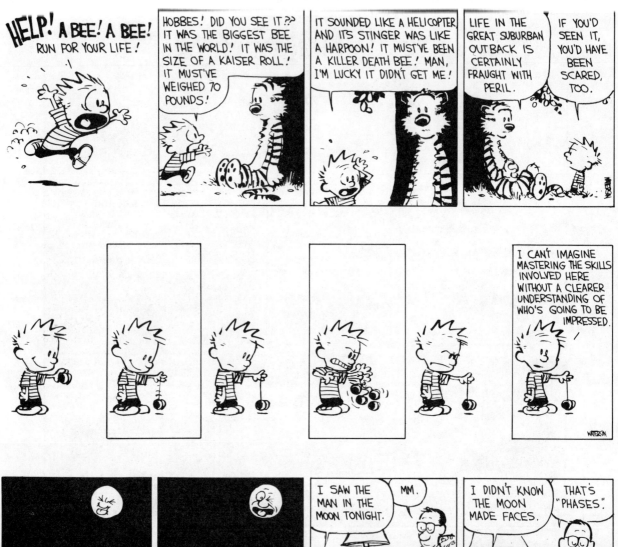

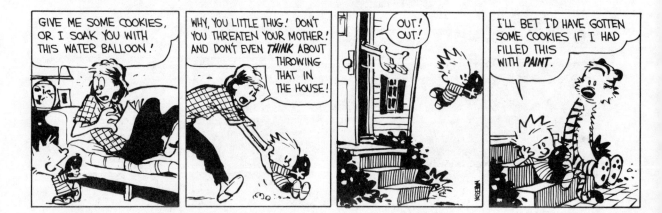

92

IT'S JULY ALREADY! OH NO! OH NO!

WHAT HAPPENED TO JUNE?! SUMMER VACATION IS SLIPPING THROUGH OUR FINGERS LIKE GRAINS OF SAND!

IT'S GOING TOO FAST! WE'VE GOT TO HOARD OUR FREEDOM AND HAVE MORE FUN! TIME RUSHES ON! HELP! HELP!

I DON'T THINK I WANT TO BE HERE AT THE END OF AUGUST.

AAUGH! IT'S A HALF-HOUR LATER THAN IT WAS HALF AN HOUR AGO! RUN! RUN!

MOM TOOK ME TO THE LIBRARY TODAY, DAD.

THAT'S NICE. DID YOU GET OUT A BOOK?

YEP. IT'S GREAT! I HAD NO IDEA BOOKS COULD BE SO MUCH FUN.

AND YOU'LL LEARN THINGS, TOO.

I'LL SAY! MY BOOK SAYS THAT THIS ONE WASP LAYS ITS EGG ON A SPIDER, SO WHEN THE EGG HATCHES, THE LARVA EATS THE SPIDER, SAVING THE VITAL ORGANS FOR LAST, SO THE SPIDER STAYS ALIVE WHILE IT'S BEING DEVOURED!

GROSS, HUH?

ISN'T THERE A STREET CORNER WHERE HE COULD HANG OUT INSTEAD?

AND COLOR PICTURES, TOO! WANT TO SEE 'EM?

I'M DESTINED FOR GREATNESS, I JUST KNOW IT. "CALVIN THE GREAT," THEY'LL CALL ME.

AND THINK HOW LUCKY YOU'LL BE! YOU'LL GET TO TELL EVERYONE HOW YOU KNEW ME AS A KID! WHAT A PRIVILEGE!

IN FACT, ALL THE PAPERS AND MAGAZINES WILL PROBABLY WANT TO INTERVIEW YOU TO FIND OUT WHAT I'M REALLY LIKE.

AND BOY, WILL YOU HAVE TO COUGH UP TO KEEP ME QUIET.

AND WHAT'S THAT SUPPOSED TO MEAN?!

94

98

WELL, THERE'S NO DELAYING THE INEVITABLE. LET'S GET IN THE CAR.

WHERE ARE WE GOING?

THE SAME PLACE WE GO *EVERY* SUMMER : CAMPING ON SOME DESOLATE ROCK AT THE END OF THE EARTH.

AGAIN?

YEP. THIS IS HOW DAD LIKES TO UNWIND.

WITH EVERYONE COMPLAINING?

RIGHT. HE LIKES TO WATCH US ALL SUFFER.

LOOK, DAD, THERE'S A TOWN COMING UP. SEE THE SIGN?

WHY DON'T WE PULL OFF, FIND A NICE MOTEL AND JUST STAY *THERE* FOR OUR VACATION? WE COULD SWIM IN THE POOL AND HAVE AIR CONDITIONING AND COLOR CABLE TV AND ROOM SERVICE!

NO ONE WOULD HAVE TO KNOW WE DIDN'T CAMP! *I* WOULDN'T TELL ANYONE! WE COULD EVEN GO TO THE STORE, BUY A BIG FISH, TAKE YOUR PICTURE WITH IT, AND SAY YOU CAUGHT IT! CAN'T WE, DAD? CAN'T WE TURN OFF HERE?

YES, LET'S!

NOW DON'T *YOU* START!

TA DA! WE'RE HERE!

GOOD OL' "ITCHY ISLAND," HOME OF THE NUCLEAR MOSQUITOES.

BUG BITES BUILD CHARACTER.

YEAH, AND LAST YEAR YOU SAID DIARRHEA BUILDS CHARACTER.

SO THINK WHAT A FINE YOUNG MAN YOU'RE GROWING UP TO BE.

...IF ALL THIS CHARACTER DOESN'T KILL ME FIRST.

THAT REMINDS ME, OPEN THE DUFFEL BAG AND GET OUT THE SPAM.

IF THE CANOE ISN'T HERE IN THE MORNING, IT MEANS HOBBES AND I STRUCK OUT FOR HOME.

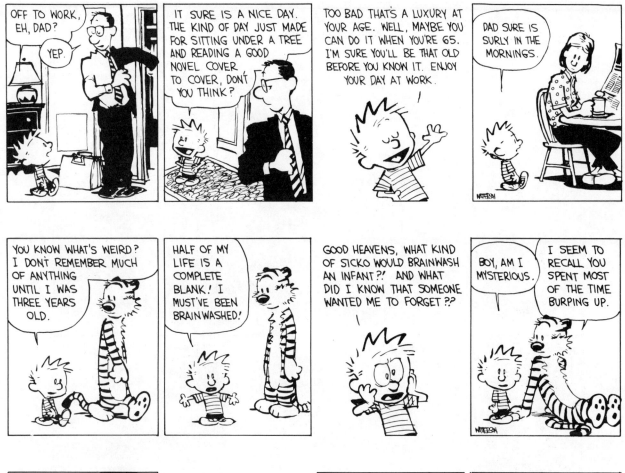

108

109

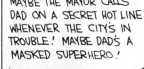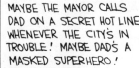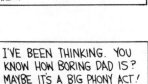

114

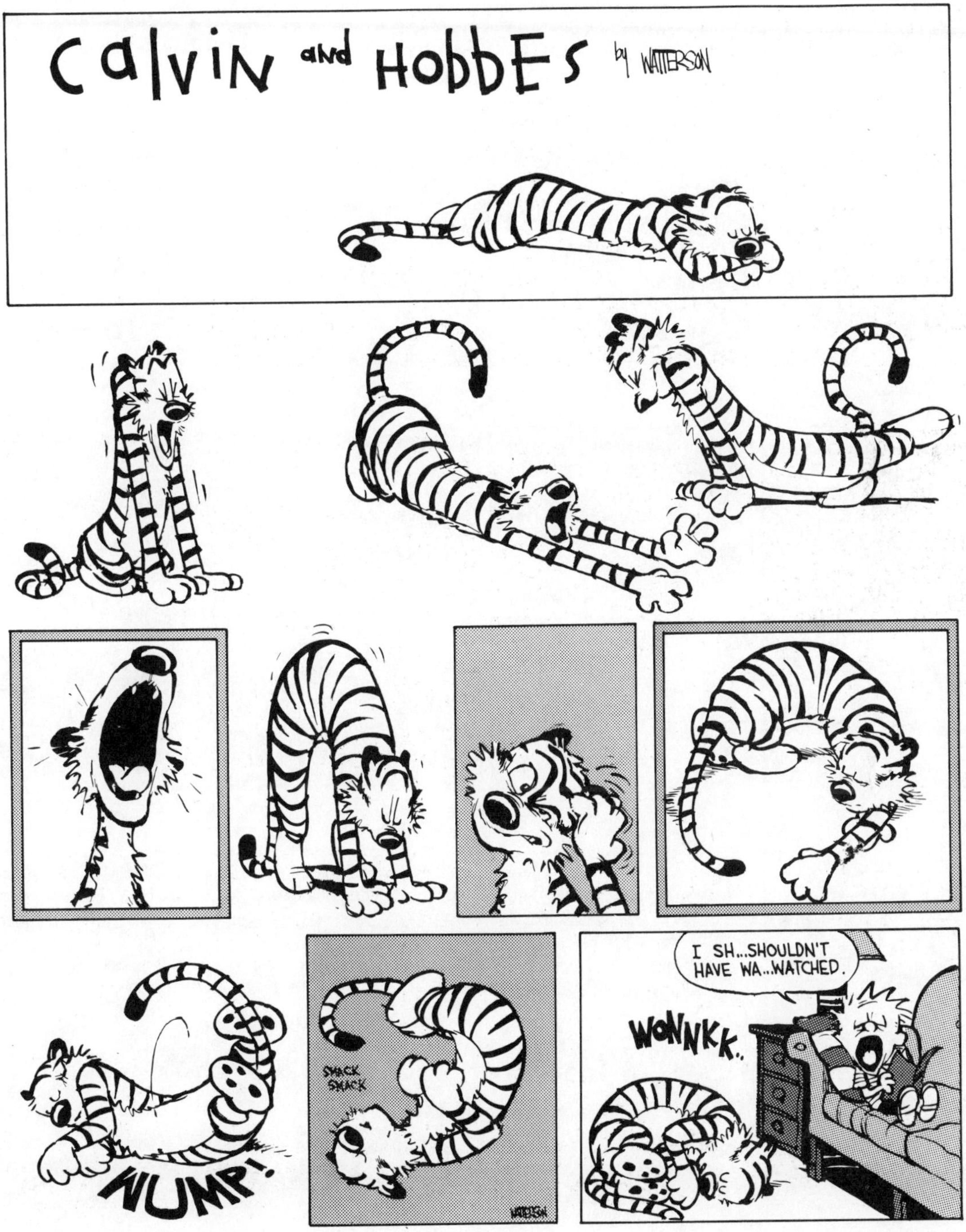
Calvin and HobbEs by WATTERSON
NUMP!
SMACK
SMACK
WATTERSON
I SH...SHOULDN'T HAVE WA...WATCHED.
WONNKK..

116

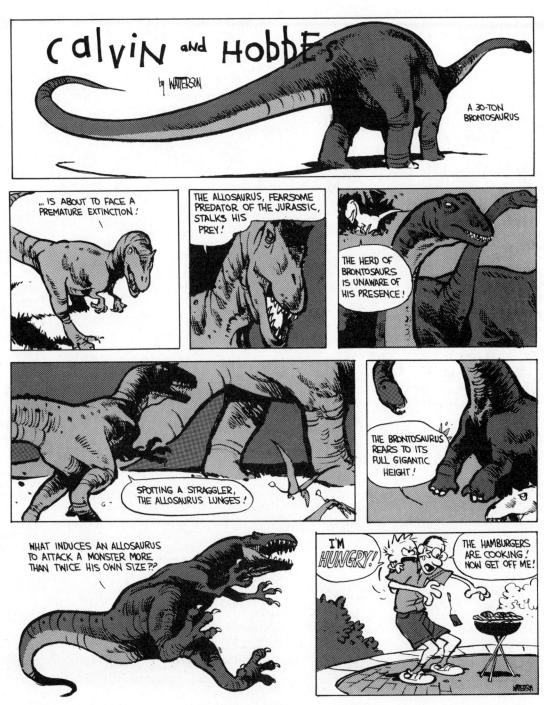

119

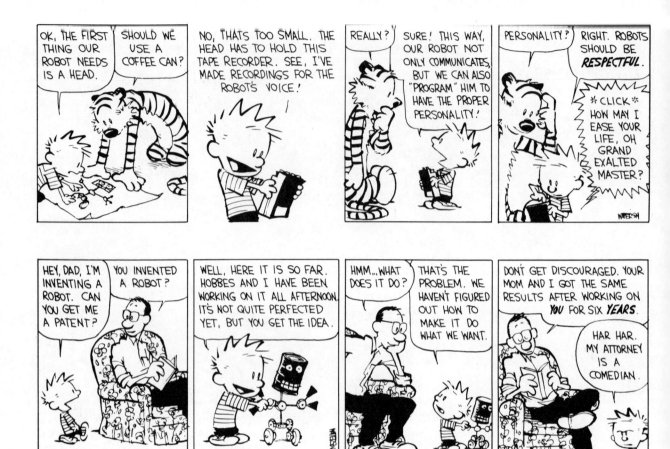

UH OH, CALVIN THE REPTILE IS IN TROUBLE!

AS AN ECTOTHERM, HIS BODY RELIES ON THE ENVIRONMENT TO WARM OR COOL ITS TEMPERATURE.

NOW THAT IT'S COLDER OUTSIDE, CALVIN'S BODY TEMPERATURE FALLS AND HE BECOMES SLUGGISH! HE'LL GO INTO TORPOR IF HE CAN'T FIND A WARM PLACE TO LIE!

LEAVE THE THERMOSTAT ALONE, AND PUT ON A SWEATER IF YOU'RE COLD.

I...I DON'T HAVE THE EN..ENERGY!

I HEARD THAT BIG CATS DON'T PURR.

THAT'S TRUE. WE'RE TOO FIERCE AND FEROCIOUS. WE DON'T EVER PURR.

WELL WHAT DO YOU CALL THE NOISE YOU MAKE WHEN YOU GET YOUR TUMMY RUBBED?!

GROWLING FRIENDLY-LIKE.

CALVIN, YOUR MOM AND I LOOKED OVER YOUR REPORT CARD, AND WE THINK YOU COULD BE DOING BETTER.

BUT I DON'T LIKE SCHOOL.

WHY NOT? YOU LIKE TO READ AND YOU LIKE TO LEARN. I KNOW YOU DO.

I MEAN, YOU'VE READ EVERY DINOSAUR BOOK EVER WRITTEN, AND YOU'VE LEARNED A LOT, RIGHT? READING AND LEARNING ARE FUN.

YEAH..

SO WHY DON'T YOU LIKE SCHOOL?

WE DON'T READ ABOUT DINOSAURS.

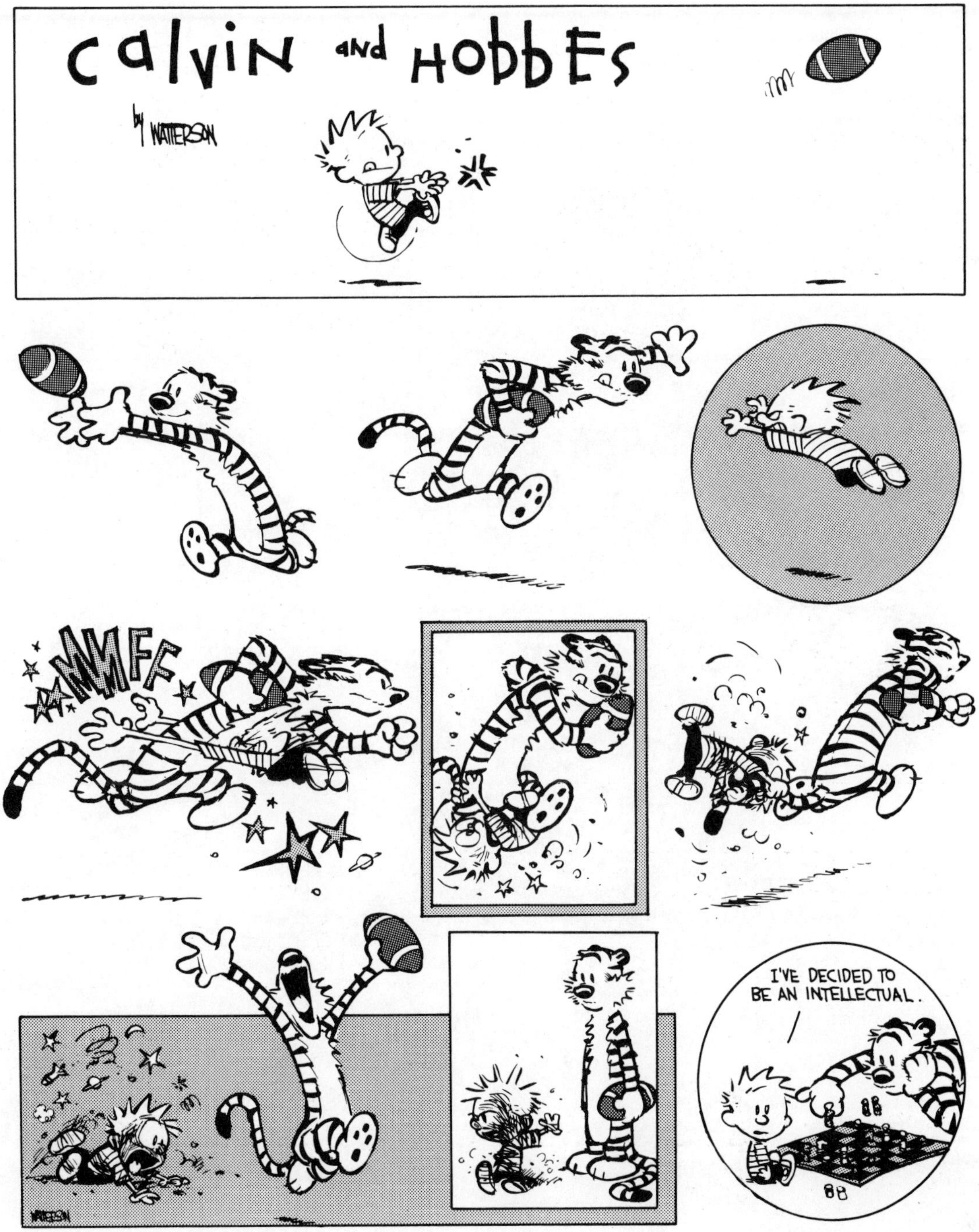
calvin and HOBBES
by WATTERSON
WMFF
I'VE DECIDED TO BE AN INTELLECTUAL.

The End